ENRICHING RELATIONSHIPS

BONNIE BUDZOWSKI

Harold Shaw Publishers
Wheaton, Illinois

Copyright © 1993 by Bonnie Budzowski

Unless otherwise indicated, all Scripture quotations are taken from The Holy Bible: New International Version. Copyright 1973, 1978, 1984 by the International Bible Society. Used by permission of Zondervan Publishing House. All rights reserved.

All rights reserved. No part of this book may be reproduced or transmitted in any form or by any means, electronic or mechanical, including photocopying, recording, or any information storage and retrieval system without written permission from Harold Shaw Publishers, Box 567, Wheaton, Illinois 60189. Printed in the United States of America.

ISBN 0-87788-214-2

Cover graphics by John Seid

Cover illustration © 1993 by David LaPlaca

99 98 97 96 95 94 93

10 9 8 7 6 5 4 3 2 1

Contents

How to Use This Discussion Guide	5
Introduction	7
Study One/Living in God's Light Ephesians 4:17-32	9
Study Two/Living to Please God Mark 3:1-6; Acts 1:1-4,13-31; Romans 12:9-21	13
Study Three/Balancing Truth and Love Mark 10:17-22; John 8:1-11	17
Study Four/Sinless Anger John 2:13-17; Luke 15:11-24	21
Study Five/Tamed Tongues Psalm 15; Proverbs 12:14-19; Colossians 3:12-17	25
Study Six/Foundations of Forgiveness John 20:19-29; 21:1-19	29
Study Seven/Barriers to Forgiveness Luke 22:24-27; James 3:13-18	33
Study Eight/Honesty with God Psalm 73	36
Leader's Notes	40
Sources and Suggested Reading	48

How to Use This Discussion Guide

NetWork Discussion Guides are designed for "people on the move." A typical group might use these studies during a lunch break, as part of a fellowship evening in a home, or in a Sunday school class.

Each study is designed to take about 30 minutes to complete. If you have more than 30 minutes, your group can spend valuable time praying and fellowshiping together.

NetWork studies address important contemporary issues from a biblical perspective. Their ultimate goal is to help you put God's Word into practice in your life. To do this, each study includes three segments.

OPENING IT UP

The study begins with a discussion launcher. This might be a short case study, a provocative quote, or a problem-posing story intended to spark discussion and draw out personal opinion. Spend about 5 minutes on this opener. It will help you to focus on the theme of the study and will help participants to become involved in the discussion.

THINKING IT THROUGH

This section focuses on a Scripture passage, with 4-6 questions that draw out the facts and the meaning of the passage. These thoughtful questions should take about 15 minutes. Background notes on each passage are part of the Leader's Notes.

MAKING IT HAPPEN

This section brings immediacy and concreteness to the issue, with suggestions for life application. Here, group members are encouraged to ask, "So what? What am I going to do about obeying this Scripture in my home or at my job?" Spend about 10 minutes on this important wrap-up.

Each study also features a Journal Entry for follow-up at home. This is another way to make truth personal and active.

You will find additional suggestions for leading the group and helpful notes on each Scripture passage in the Leader's Notes at the back of the guide.

Introduction

In today's society, each of us has a myriad of relationships: we relate to our families, our co-workers, our bosses and subordinates, our neighbors, fellow church members, and friends. Most of us long for these relationships to be warm and fulfilling, reflective of the love of God working through us and among us. Yet, it is common for relationships to be fraught with frustration and disillusionment. We struggle with anger over a sister's consistent insensitivity; we wonder if we should confront our boss over an integrity issue at work; and we choke on words of forgiveness we know are needed by an old friend.

The Bible has much to say about relationships, especially those within the fellowship of the church. Some of the teaching is found in beautiful words like the "love chapter" in 1 Corinthians 13. At times these words make us feel worse, because we are clue-less as to how to attain such heights. Often the path is found in the actual relationships described on the pages of the Bible: those Jesus had with his disciples or the people he met on his journeys or described in parables. These studies will point to biblical examples as well as to direct teaching. May the light of the Lord's Word shine grace upon our lives.

☐ Study One

LIVING IN GOD'S LIGHT

Ephesians 4:17-32

OPENING IT UP

The syndicated columnist, Sydney Harris, tells of accompanying his friend to a newsstand. His friend greeted the newsman very courteously, but in return received gruff and discourteous service. Accepting the newspaper that was shoved rudely in his direction, the friend smiled politely and wished the newsman a nice weekend. As the two friends walked down the street, the columnist asked:

"Does he always treat you so rudely?"
"Yes, unfortunately he does."
"And are you always so polite and friendly to him?"
"Yes, I am."
"Why are you so nice to him when he is so unfriendly to you?"
"Because I don't want *him* to decide how *I'm* going to act."

The suggestion is that the "fully human" person is "his own person," that he does not bend to every wind that blows, that he is not at the mercy of all the pettiness, the meanness, the impatience and anger of others. Atmospheres do not transform him as much as he transforms them.—John Powell, *Why Am I Afraid to Tell You Who I Am?*

In relationships, how are you prone to act or react?

THINKING IT THROUGH

1. Read Ephesians 4:17-32. How does Paul use the imagery of clothing in this passage?

2. In this teaching about the new life, what is the significance of Paul's focus on relationship rather than on religious practices?

3. Review verses 25-32. Using your own words, briefly describe Paul's teaching on the subjects listed below. Note the actions Paul says we should "put off" (stop doing) as well as the ones we should "put on" (start doing).

Speech with or toward others

Anger

Finances

Forgiveness

LIVING IN GOD'S LIGHT

4. In verse 31, Paul prohibits bitterness, rage, anger, brawling, slander, and malice. How do you understand this string of words? If you can, give examples.

5. In what ways have you seen relationships give a foothold to the devil or grieve the Holy Spirit?

MAKING IT HAPPEN

> Truth and love are two necessary ingredients for any relationship with integrity. Love—because all positive relationships begin with friendship, appreciation, respect. And truth—because no relationship of trust can long grow from dishonesty, deceit, betrayal; it springs up from solid stuff of integrity.
>
> "Confrontation plus caring brings growth just as judgment plus grace brings salvation," says Howard Clinebell, Jr., a well-known pastoral counselor.
>
> These are the two arms of genuine relationship; Confrontation with truth; Affirmation with love.—David Augsburger, *Caring Enough to Confront*

Are you better at "confrontation with truth" or "affirmation with love"? What can you do to develop in the weaker area?

According to David Augsburger, "You can be angry (at behaviors) and loving (toward persons) at the same time." Give an example or describe how this might work.

In what ways are you responsible to ensure that your church reflects Paul's teaching on relationships?

Journal Entry

> Do nothing out of selfish ambition or vain conceit, but in humility consider others better than yourselves. Each of you should look not only to your own interests, but also to the interests of others. Your attitude should be the same as that of Christ Jesus: Who, being in very nature God, did not count equality with God something to be grasped, but made himself nothing, taking the very nature of a servant, being made in human likeness. And being found in appearance as a man, he humbled himself and became obedient to death—even death on a cross! Therefore God exalted him to the highest place . . .—Philippians 2:3-9

Take a few minutes to identify all your major relationships at this time. Make a list of them. Reflect on Jesus' attitude toward others and pray about your various relationships. Tell God about specific changes you need to make over the course of this Bible study.

☐ STUDY TWO

LIVING TO PLEASE GOD

Mark 3:1-6; Acts 1:1-4,13-31; Romans 12:9-21

OPENING IT UP

What is Jesus like? Here are two contrasting representations:

> Away in a manger, no crib for a bed,
> The little Lord Jesus laid down His sweet head.
> The stars in the sky all looked where he lay,
> The little Lord Jesus, asleep on the hay.
> —James R. Murray, "Away in a Manger"

> We may note . . . that He [Jesus] was never regarded as a mere moral teacher. He did not produce that effect on any of the people who actually met Him. He produced mainly three effects—Hatred—Terror—Adoration.—C.S. Lewis, *God in the Dock*

Which of these portrayals of Jesus do you think is closer to the biblical truth? Explain your answers.

THINKING IT THROUGH

1. Read Mark 3:1-6. In this account, Jesus deliberately acts in a way that is contrary to the customs and wishes of the religious authorities of his day. What emotions did Jesus experience (verse 5)?

2. What principle(s) do you think motivated Jesus' actions?

3. Read Acts 4:1-3,13-31. Here the apostles refuse to obey the religious authorities. What principle(s) do you think motivated their response?

4. When the apostles pray for themselves, what is their primary request?

5. Read Romans 12:9-21. What relationship goals are outlined here? According to this passage, how should conflict be managed?

LIVING TO PLEASE GOD 15

MAKING IT HAPPEN

Write down some possible endings to the following sentence:

As a Christian, it is acceptable for me to make choices that displease others when:

Placed in a difficult situation, are you more prone to remain in harmony with others at the expense of your Christian principles or to defend your principles at the expense of another's dignity and self-esteem? If possible give an example.

What alternate response is outlined in Romans 12:9-21? How are we to treat those with whom we differ when we must make a stand because of our convictions?

> Cowardice asks, Is it safe?
> Expediency asks, Is it polite?
> Vanity asks, Is it popular? but
> Conscience asks, Is it right?
> —William Morley Penshon

Reflect on the responses to conflict in the three Scripture passages studied in this lesson. What practical steps do you need to take in order to respond biblically to conflict?

Journal Entry

Look again at the list you made of your various relationships. What challenges do each of these relationships present to you? Ask God to give you courage to live boldly for him while you treat others with genuine love.

☐ STUDY THREE

BALANCING TRUTH AND LOVE

Mark 10:17-22; John 8:1-11

OPENING IT UP

Sally was in an accident that put her car out of commission for many weeks. Her leg was injured, making it difficult for her to use public transportation. Quite shaken by the accident, Sally needed the help and support of her friends. Although informed about the accident, Jean, a friend from her Bible study group, never called, sent a card, or offered to help. The other members of the group were helpful to Sally in a number of ways.

Sally was angry and frustrated, but she never said anything to Jean or anyone else. Still, after the accident, Sally stopped calling Jean on a personal basis. Then she felt upset because Jean didn't seem to notice. After that, everything Jean said and did annoyed her. A fuse of anger and irritability was burning slowly and steadily within Sally.

One day Jean forgot a book she had promised to bring to the Bible study for Sally. Sally turned red in the face, raised her voice, and gave a long, angry lecture about what an irresponsible and horrible person Jean was. Neither Jean nor anyone else in the group had any idea what had provoked Sally's response. Things were very tense after that.

Have you ever had an experience like the one described here? As you see it, what went wrong with Sally and Jean, and what can be done to help them?

THINKING IT THROUGH

1. Read Mark 10:17-22. Describe the balance of truth and love in Jesus' encounter with the rich young ruler.

2. Read John 8:1-11. Describe the balance of truth and love in this encounter between our Lord and the woman caught in adultery.

3. What do you imagine happened to the rich young ruler and the adulterous woman?

4. Given the information we have, how would you evaluate Jesus' success or lack thereof in these encounters?

BALANCING TRUTH AND LOVE

MAKING IT HAPPEN

> Brothers, if someone is caught in a sin, you who are spiritual should restore him gently. But watch yourself, or you also may be tempted.—Galatians 6:1
>
> So watch yourselves. If your brother sins, rebuke him, and if he repents, forgive him.—Luke 17:3

There are five basic styles for handling conflict:

- Attacking
- Withdrawing
- Smoothing it over
- Compromising
- Balancing truth with love

Identify your predominant style. How did you come to develop this pattern?

In what ways has your style for dealing with conflict been constructive or destructive for you? How do you feel it compares to the biblical model?

Give an example of a situation in which you have seen someone balance the truth with love. What can you learn from this example?

> GUIDELINES FOR BALANCING THE TRUTH WITH LOVE
>
> Describe facts and the other person's actual behavior, remembering that you are not in a position to judge another's motives or intentions.
>
> Present your feelings and the impact of the situation on you, but do not blame the other for your feelings.
>
> Present your feelings clearly and concisely. Do not overwhelm the other person with an avalanche of words or emotion.
>
> Let the person know what you would like out of the situation, but do not demand compliance. Seek a mutual resolution.
>
> Concentrate on the current situation, avoiding broad statements about the other person's character.
>
> Express a willingness to listen to the other person's point of view.
>
> Keep your temper and present yourself with humility, recognizing that you too fall short of God's standards.

Journal Entry

Examine your relationships in light of the guidelines for balancing truth and love, paying special attention to the last point (based on Galatians 6:1). Confess any sin and ask God to help you deal with conflict in a biblical manner.

☐ Study Four

SINLESS ANGER

John 2:13-17; Luke 15:11-24

OPENING IT UP

> Theoretically, most of us would accept the fact that emotions are neither meritorious nor sinful. Feeling frustrated, or being annoyed, or experiencing fears and anger do not make one a good or a bad person. Practically, however, most of us do not accept in our day to day living what we would accept in theory. We exercise a rather strict censorship of our emotions, repressing them into our subconscious mind. Experts in psychosomatic medicine say that the most common cause of fatigue and actual sickness is the repression of emotions. The fact is that there are emotions to which we do not want to admit. We are ashamed of our fears, or we feel guilty because of our anger . . . —John Powell, *Why Am I Afraid to Tell You Who I Am?*

Do you feel guilty or sinful when you experience angry feelings? Where do you think such guilt comes from?

THINKING IT THROUGH

1. Read John 2:13-17. Recall the story of the man with the withered hand (Study Two, page 13). What circumstances provoked Jesus to anger? What do these passages reveal about his character and priorities?

> Anger is an emotion that appears often in Scripture. It is frequently equivalent to wrath, and the person most often described as angry is God Himself. In Ezekiel 16:26 God says, "You engaged in prostitution with the Egyptians . . . and provoked me to anger with your increasing promiscuity." Mark tells us "[Jesus] looked around at them in anger . . . deeply distressed at their stubborn hearts" (Mark 3:5).
>
> God has anger. Jesus has anger. We are made to image God and are being progressively conformed to the image of His Son. Imaging God includes having anger. Our task as Christians is not to rid ourselves of all anger, but to have appropriate anger in a godly way.—James Hurley, *RTS Ministry*
>
> The LORD, the LORD, the compassionate and gracious God, slow to anger, abounding in love and faithfulness—Exodus 34:6
>
> Everyone should be quick to listen, slow to speak and slow to become angry, for man's anger does not bring about the righteous life that God desires.—James 1:19-20

2. Knowing that God does get angry, contrast human anger and God's anger.

3. What does it mean to be slow to anger?

4. Skim Luke 15:11-24. Then read verses 25-32 more carefully. Choose three words or phrases to describe the elder brother's attitude. What are his spoken or unspoken demands?

MAKING IT HAPPEN

Imagine that the elder brother in the parable decides to obey the command, "In your anger, do not sin" (Ephesians 4:26). What happens now?

When you are angry, what are you usually demanding?

What are the differences between a person who is slow to anger and a person who denies or represses anger?

H. Norman Wright says it is possible to be angry in a "Christian way," by staying within the guidelines below.

   1. The anger must be directed at something wrong or evil.

2. It must be controlled and not a heated, uncontrolled passion.
3. There must be no hatred, malice, or resentment.

How does this compare with the anger you experience? Is there anything you would like to change or add to the above guidelines?

What changes in your behavior do the guidelines suggest?

Journal Entry

Describe the circumstances in which you are most likely to be quick to anger. Think about the week ahead of you and pray that you will be slow to anger in specific circumstances and with specific people you will encounter.

☐ STUDY FIVE

TAMED TONGUES

Psalm 15; Proverbs 12:14-19; Colossians 3:12-17

OPENING IT UP

> To act as if another does not exist is a more hostile act than to slap his face. In the latter action one at least acknowledges his presence. The silent treatment is an extremely powerful weapon of aggression.—C. Fitzsimons Allison, *Guilt, Anger & God*

> Some individuals . . . deal with their emotions like trading stamps. They save up each little irritation as though it were a stamp. They accumulate many stamps and, finally, when something happens that is the last straw, they blow up . . . —H. Norman Wright, *Communication: The Key to Your Marriage*

Our patterns of speech reveal a lot about how we've learned to deal with conflict. What experiences have you had with the conflict strategies described above?

THINKING IT THROUGH

> If anyone considers himself religious and yet does not keep a tight rein on his tongue, he deceives himself and his religion is worthless.—James 1:26

1. Read Psalm 15. According to this psalm, how much do words have to do with being a holy person?

2. What is the main characteristic of godly speech as described here?

3. Read Proverbs 12:14-19. What do these verses say, positively and negatively, about the power of words?

4. How might a person's *words* and *works* be related (verse 14)?

5. Read Colossians 3:12-17. Notice the focus on Jesus Christ in these verses. To what extent is the choice of words a matter of personal decision or a supernatural work of God?

6. How important is the quality of thankfulness in a person who chooses words wisely?

MAKING IT HAPPEN

> Pleasant words are a honeycomb, sweet to the soul and healing to the bones.—Proverbs 16:24

Do you work as hard at accomplishing positive things in your speech as you do at avoiding negative things? Why or why not?

Think of someone you know whose speech is positive and edifying for others. What ingredients give this person success in this area?

> "I messages" are honest, clear, confessional. "I messages" own my anger, my responsibility, my demands without placing blame. Note the contrast between honest confession and distorted rejection.

I Messages	You Messages
I am angry.	You make me angry.
I feel rejected.	You're judging and rejecting me.
I don't like the wall between us.	You're building a wall between us.
I don't like blaming or being blamed.	You're blaming everything on me.
I want the freedom to say yes or no.	You're trying to run my life.
I want respectful friendship with you again.	You've got to respect me or you're not my friend.

—David Augsburger, *Caring Enough to Confront*

Proverbs 15:1 says, "A gentle answer turns away wrath, but a harsh word stirs up anger." How might "I messages" and honest statements meet the criterion of a "gentle" answer?

In Matthew 12:34, Jesus teaches that "out of the overflow of the heart the mouth speaks." Based on the words you speak, are you satisfied with the condition of your heart? If not, list specific steps you need to take in order for your words to be truthful, constructive, and edifying.

Journal Entry

Consider the way you speak to a close friend or family member. Think specifically of things in this person's behavior that consistently upset you. Formulate "I messages" to communicate honestly in these areas. Now prayerfully make a plan for adding positive, edifying speech in your relationship with this person.

☐ STUDY SIX

FOUNDATIONS OF FORGIVENESS

John 20:19-29; 21:1-19

OPENING IT UP

Imagine yourself as one of the disciples just after Jesus' death. You are one of the group who, in the moment of danger, abandoned your master. It started when Judas, a close disciple, betrayed him. In the end, only John and some devoted women dared to watch the crucifixion. The rest of you fled. Now you are hiding in a locked room in Jerusalem, unsure of what to do next.

How do you feel about your behavior toward Jesus?

What is your estimation of your own character at this point?

If you imagine yourself as Peter, what emotions are you experiencing?

THINKING IT THROUGH

1. Read John 20:19-29. This is the disciples' first encounter with Jesus since they had abandoned their master during his passion. What is surprising about Jesus' message to them?

2. Jesus repeats "Peace be with you" three times. What would Jesus' message of peace mean to the disciples at this time?

3. Read John 21:1-19. The time period between Peter's denial of Jesus and this incident is forty days or less. Describe what has happened in the relationship between Jesus and Peter in the meantime.

4. How does Jesus affirm his forgiveness to Peter?

MAKING IT HAPPEN

When you have asked forgiveness for a major sin, are you able to approach Jesus with the eagerness with which Peter did? List any barriers that get in your way.

FOUNDATIONS OF FORGIVENESS

> Therefore, as God's chosen people, holy and dearly loved, clothe yourselves with compassion, kindness, humility, gentleness and patience. Bear with each other and forgive whatever grievances you may have against one another. Forgive as the Lord forgave you.—Colossians 3:12-13
>
> Accept one another, then, just as Christ accepted you, in order to bring praise to God.—Romans 15:7

The foundation of our forgiveness toward others must be found in the forgiveness we receive in Christ. What happens in our relationships with others if we do not feel accepted or fully forgiven by Christ?

How might our acceptance of one another "bring praise to God" (Romans 15:7)?

> ... the greatest form of grace-talk we may practice today is the simple phrase, "Will you forgive me?" Built into this almost miraculous formula is grace as a gift of forgiveness that is beyond our human capabilities, plus an awareness of the shared ground for all forgiving: the forgiveness we have received ... The grace to forgive affirms our worth while it cements our bonds.—Jerry Harvill, *Discipleship Journal*

What changes must you make in order to forgive fully as Christ has forgiven you?

Journal Entry

> A forgiving heart offers to others a glimpse of the mysterious wonder of God's character. The energy to serve others a taste of God will be no greater than our own taste of God's forgiveness.—Dan Allender, *Discipleship Journal*

List specific sins for which the Lord has forgiven you. Express your gladness at the Lord's forgiveness. Ask the Lord to release you from any feelings of shame that remain.

□ STUDY SEVEN

BARRIERS TO FORGIVENESS

Luke 22:24-27; James 3:13-18

OPENING IT UP

> First, don't forgive everything that annoys you. There are some pains we ought not to forgive for two reasons: (1) they're not serious enough; and (2) they're not things for which another person is responsible, such as depression.
>
> A man once came to me and said, "My wife has been depressed for three years. Now she's just a couch potato who leaves the couch only to fill her stomach. I can't take it. How can I forgive her?"
>
> So I asked, "Would you forgive her if she broke her leg? It's the same thing. You don't forgive. You bear, you wait, you suffer along with her."
>
> Patience is not the same thing as forgiving.—Lewis Smedes, *Marriage Partnership*

What is your reaction to Smedes' distinction between patience and forgiveness?

THINKING IT THROUGH

1. Read Luke 22:24-27. Compare Jesus' attitude toward others with that of the disciples' attitude. What do these attitudes have to do with forgiveness?

2. Read James 3:13-18. Summarize the characteristics of wisdom that is from above, and wisdom that is earthly.

3. Using the Scripture passages from Luke and James, formulate a list of barriers that can prevent us from forgiving others as Christ forgave us.

4. Which of these barriers cause you the most problems?

MAKING IT HAPPEN

> Who is a God like you,
> who pardons sin and forgives
> the transgression
> of the remnant of his inheritance?
> You do not stay angry forever
> but delight to show mercy.
> —Micah 7:18

BARRIERS TO FORGIVENESS

In contrast to God, who "does not stay angry forever," humans are prone to practice bitterness and resentment. In what ways have you found these practices to be self-destructive, in yourself and others?

What have you found to be helpful in your struggles with resentment?

> Hebrews 12:15 states that a root of bitterness can spring up and cause trouble, causing many to be defiled. You cannot nurture the bitterness plant and at the same time keep it concealed. The bitter root bears fruit. You may think you can hide it . . . live with it . . . "grin and bear it," but you cannot. Slowly, inexorably, that sharp, cutting edge of unforgiveness will work its way to the surface. The poison seedling will find insidious ways to cut into others. Ironically, the one who suffers most is the one who lashes out at those around him.—Charles R. Swindoll, *The Seasons of Life*

Journal Entry

Examine your life for resentment and unreasonable demands on others, asking God to enable you to grant full forgiveness. If this is not possible at the moment, make a prayerful list of steps necessary in order to reach the point of granting full forgiveness.

☐ STUDY EIGHT

HONESTY WITH GOD

Psalm 73

OPENING IT UP

I know a church which is an unusually lively place with an unconventional tradition of honesty facing the deep and unpleasant hurts of its people. Therapists send their patients there for the warm skillful help given in the various parish groups. The clergyman in charge observed with all modesty that he honestly believed they were dealing with interpersonal anger as well as any group in the metropolis but "we don't handle cosmic anger very well." Far more serious than the anger between and among persons is this anger toward God . . .—C. Fitzsimons Allison, *Guilt, Anger & God*

Do you think it is okay to be angry toward God? Why or why not?

What would happen if you expressed anger toward God in your church?

THINKING IT THROUGH

1. Read Psalm 73. How would you describe the psalmist's gripe with God?

2. What emotions are most prominent? To whom does the psalmist address these emotions?

3. In what specific ways do you see the psalmist turning toward or away from God?

4. The psalmist's circumstances do not change by the end of this prayer, yet his inner conflict is resolved. What happened?

MAKING IT HAPPEN

As part of Israel's prayerbook, this psalm is an example of a righteous prayer. How does it teach you to pray, especially in times of distress?

> It's easy to acknowledge God and rejoice when everything is going great. It's another thing, however, to do so when our lives are interrupted by the unexpected. Then it's often difficult to see God working.
>
> We live in a generation that feels that if we can just understand something enough, we can control it. We feel that God has an obligation to explain his reasons for things that happen to us. We argue when we don't get answers, and we become bitter when things don't go our way.
>
> Throughout Scripture God allows his people to ventilate their feelings. We're even told, "If any of you lacks wisdom, let him ask of God, who gives to all liberally and without reproach" (James 1:5a). And yet, God is not required to give us an explanation. He wants us to trust him.—Dr. Richard Fowler, *Today's Better Life*

Chuck Swindoll, telling a story of a woman who lost her son in a DC-4 plane crash, says, "Mrs. Chambers stopped asking *Why* when she saw the *Who* behind the scene. All other sounds are muffled when we claim His absolute sovereignty." How does this match the psalmist's experience?

How do you feel about the fact that God often does not provide an explanation?

HONESTY WITH GOD

> The psalmists of old often referred to this fragile interconnectedness between our spirituality and our emotions. One psalmist laments, "Why, O Lord, do you stand far off? Why do you hide yourself in times of trouble?" (Psalm 10:1). A few psalms later, David beseeches God, "How long, O Lord? Will you forget me forever? How long will you hide your face from me?" (Psalm 13:1). God had not changed—but pain temporarily eclipsed the reality of His presence.
>
> ... When the psalmists poured out their honest feelings about God's "distance" when they were in pain, I believe God was neither shocked nor offended by their struggles with Him. I think He understood and accepted them right where they were, just as He accepts me when I question Him.—Becky Brodin, *Discipleship Journal*

Besides anger, what emotions occur in your relationship with God that you find embarrassing or difficult to express?

What do you think are the biblical parameters for expressing anger to God?

Journal Entry

Write a prayer about a current situation in your life that reflects what you have learned about honest prayer from Psalm 73.

Leader's Notes

As leader of your group, one of your key roles is to keep the discussion on target. You don't need to be an expert or an answer person—your responsibility is to ask, not tell. The questions in the discussion guide will help you to facilitate meaningful discussion.

NetWork Discussion Guides provide spaces between questions for jotting down responses, comments, and related questions you would like to raise in the group. Each group member should have a copy of the guide and may take a turn in leading your group.

This studyguide is based on the **New International Version** of the Bible. Encourage group members to use any accurate, modern translation as the basis for study and discussion.

Preparing to Lead

1. Read and study the Bible passage and related material thoroughly beforehand, asking God to help you understand and apply the passage to your own life.

2. Pray for each member of your group, asking God to prepare each one for the life-changing truth of the study.

3. Familiarize yourself with the leader's notes for the study you are leading. These notes provide you with background information and comments about some of the questions. Use the space below the questions to make notes of helpful ideas.

LEADER'S NOTES

Leading the Study

1. Begin (and end) the study promptly.

2. Lead in prayer or ask someone ahead of time to open with prayer.

3. Explain that your study format will be a discussion, not a lecture. Encourage everyone to participate, but don't push those who are hesitant to speak the first few sessions.

4. Read the discussion launcher (OPENING IT UP) out loud and discuss the accompanying question.

5. Read the Bible passage aloud, or ask a volunteer to read it. Then ask each question in the THINKING IT THROUGH section, encouraging all to participate. Don't be afraid of silence. Allow time for thoughtful answers.

6. Don't answer your own questions. If necessary, repeat or rephrase questions until they are clearly understood.

7. If a question comes up that you can't answer, don't be afraid to admit you're baffled! Assign the topic as a research project for someone to report on the next time you meet.

8. When tangents are introduced, bring the discussion back to the topic at hand. Sometimes, of course, tangents are important. Be sensitive to the Holy Spirit and to the needs of your group.

9. Be sure to leave adequate time for the application questions in MAKING IT HAPPEN. The goal of these studies is changed lives!

10. End your discussion with specific, personal prayer for each other, asking God to help you obey the Scripture you studied.

Study One/Living in God's Light

Purpose: To provide a basic foundation for a Christian understanding of relationships. Topics introduced by this passage of Scripture (truth, anger, speech, forgiveness, and bitterness) will be explored in detail in later studies.

Question 2. A vital relationship with God is always lived out in our relationships with others.

Question 3. Note especially the following: 1) we are to speak truthful words, but only such that are edifying; 2) anger, if handled correctly, is not sin; 3) we are to give rather than hoard resources; and 4) our forgiveness of one another is to mirror God's forgiveness of us.

Question 4. Perhaps Paul's stringing these words together indicates that they all spring from the same sinful motives. I think the anger listed here is anger that is harbored, as opposed to anger that is quickly resolved as in verse 26. Verse 32 provides the positive alternative to the prohibited behavior in verse 31.

Question 5. To nurse anger is to become bitter and resentful and give a foothold to the devil. Yet, suppression of anger is unhealthy and can lead to a variety of problems. Paul's command not to let the sun go down on your anger is not a command to pretend that anger is not there. It is an encouragement to work through the anger directly rather than allow it to fester.

Study Two/Living to Please God

Purpose: To respond to conflict in a way that pleases God.

Question 1. Jesus acted on the principle that love and compassion supersede the traditions of religion. The Pharisees added many of their own traditions to the Old Testament law. Conflicts between Jesus and the authorities all involved those man-made laws. The Pharisees were so caught up in their traditions that they failed to see what was good and right.

Questions 3-4. The apostles were boldly proclaiming the gospel of Jesus Christ in obedience to the Lord's command in Matthew 28:19-20. Neither the Old Testament saints, nor Jesus, nor the apostles submitted to authorities when they felt those authorities contradicted God's will. You may wish to discuss how this incident relates to Paul's command in Romans 13:1.

Question 5. Romans 12:14-18 teaches that our goal should be harmony with others. The passage also notes that this is not always a goal we can achieve (verse 18). We are required to treat others with love and patience even when we choose not to please them.

MAKING IT HAPPEN To understand how to respond to conflict, use the Bible as your standard. Obedience to God as described in his Word comes first.

Study Three/Balancing Truth and Love

Purpose: To explore ways we can follow Jesus' example of balancing truth and love in relationships.

Question 1. This account specifically notes that the Lord loved the rich young ruler. He loved him enough to speak the truth. Yet the choice of response still belonged to the ruler.

Question 2. Jesus did not condone sin in this encounter. His love was evident in his desire to be merciful even in the face of inexcusable sin. He desired to restore the woman, not condemn her. Jesus treated a woman who was much despised in her culture with great respect; respect of the other is a critical ingredient in balancing truth and love. An additional example on this topic can be found in Jesus' encounter with the woman at the well in John 4:7-26.

Questions 3-4. The Bible does not tell us the outcome of these stories. Obviously, the Lord acted in a holy and correct manner. Success in relationships is not conditional on the other person's response but on our acting with integrity, balancing truth and love.

MAKING IT HAPPEN For those wishing to pursue this topic further, I recommend David Augsburger's, *Caring Enough to Confront*, listed in the bibliography.

Regarding conflict strategies, balancing truth and love takes a great deal of time and energy. It is important in significant relationships. It may not be the most appropriate strategy in a conflict with a clerk in a store or in a highly political situation at work.

Study Four/Sinless Anger

Purpose: To explore the biblical perspective on anger.

Question 1. Many people find it hard to believe that anger is a God-given emotion. It is possible to be angry and righteous, if your motives and your expression are godly. For examples of unrighteous anger, note the motives and expressions of Jesus' opponents in these passages.

Question 3. Also see Proverbs 14:29. Among other things, being slow to anger requires acceptance of the differences in others, patience, and a servant's attitude.

Question 4. The prodigal son acted badly, and there is some cause for his brother's ill feelings. Yet, the brother seems motivated more by selfishness, bitterness, and envy than any righteousness. Note that he is not seeking to resolve his anger; he is stubbornly sulking.

MAKING IT HAPPEN James Hurley's notes about Ephesians 4:25-32 might be helpful in answering these questions:

- We may be angry without sinning. Christians are not called to deny their emotions but to manage them.

- We are not to hold on to anger. We are to recognize we are upset and deal with issues directly, preferably within the day.

- Christian maturity forgives and replaces hostility and malice with kind thoughts and actions.

It might be helpful to talk about how the brother might balance the truth with love in this situation.

Study Five/Tamed Tongues

Purpose: To explore what the Bible has to say about our speech, both in terms of what we are to avoid and in what we are to accomplish by our words.

Questions 1-2. Psalm 15 is a picture of a person who pleases God. This person's speech is characterized by truth and a commitment to his word. If he makes a promise, he keeps it, even at his own expense. His speech is not peppered with slander and reproach.

Question 3. Proverbs 12:14-19 emphasizes truth as well as self-control. A righteous person is not impulsive in speech. Note that self-control is listed as a fruit of the Spirit in Galatians 5:22-23. This is a key factor in the wounding or healing power of the tongue. Self-control is gained by prayer, by dwelling in Scripture, and by good speech habits. Memorization of Scripture can be a help.

Question 4. To illustrate this relationship, discuss the contrast of a career built on lies and one built on honesty.

MAKING IT HAPPEN When we think of biblical teaching about the tongue, we often think of commands not to slander or lie. Yet the Bible commands us to build up with our words, to edify one another.

Edifying one another does not mean to cover up conflict. Larry Crabb has said that we sometimes cover up our anger with a blanket of courtesy. Avoiding conflict often exasperates rather than solves our relational problems. It can also be a form of dishonesty. See Proverbs 28:23. We must learn to speak the truth with love.

Study Six/Foundations of Forgiveness

Purpose: To explore how our forgiveness toward others flows from our experience of God's forgiveness toward us.

Question 1. Jesus does not speak of the disciples' betrayal. He speaks words of peace and acceptance.

Question 2. In Hebrew culture the purpose of repetition is emphasis. Jesus' words assured the disciples at a time when they were fearing for their physical safety and insecure about their relationship to Jesus.

Question 3. Peter's only encounters with Jesus since his denial were the two times Jesus appeared in the upper room. Jesus' message of peace and forgiveness is so strong now that Peter feels no barrier between them, even though his sin was great and a very little time has passed. Far from feelings of shame and distance, Peter is so excited he can't wait to get to Jesus.

Question 4. Jesus allows Peter the opportunity to express his love for Jesus three times. He also gives him responsibility again, showing his trust in Peter.

MAKING IT HAPPEN In the Lord's prayer (Matthew 6:9-13), we pray that God will forgive us as we forgive others. Our ability to forgive and accept others demonstrates God's powerful forgiveness in our lives. This demonstration praises God!

Study Seven/Barriers to Forgiveness

Purpose: To identify barriers that keep us from forgiving others.

Questions 3-4. It is important to allow a full discussion of the areas that comprise the most difficulty for your group. This study focuses mostly on pride, impatience, and resentment.

MAKING IT HAPPEN Cultivating a knowledge of God's Word and character can be helpful in overcoming barriers to forgiveness. A thankful heart toward God crowds out resentful thoughts. Memorizing Scripture can also be a help. Talking with a friend who will not gossip can help us to release negative feelings. In certain instances, a person will require professional counseling in order to be free to forgive. If a person has a great deal of difficulty with this lesson, gently suggest a talk with a pastor or professional counselor. For those wishing information on the practical steps of forgiveness, I recommend the two books on this subject by David Augsburger listed in the bibliography at the back of this book.

LEADER'S NOTES **47**

Study Eight/Honesty with God

Purpose: To explore biblical parameters for expressing our emotions honestly to God.

Question 1. While the psalmist expects God to bless the righteous, it appears as though it is the wicked who prosper (verses 12-14). It seems as though holy living is in vain.

Question 2. The psalmist experiences anger, frustration, betrayal, bitterness, and confusion. Verses 15-17 answer the second part of the question.

Question 3. The psalmist speaks words of faith, even in this time of confusion. He does not act impulsively but takes his complaint into the presence of the Lord. He does not hold on to bitterness.

Question 4. See verses 15-17. In the presence of God, the psalmist realizes that God is both good and in ultimate control.

MAKING IT HAPPEN Biblical parameters for expressing emotions to God can be taken from Psalm 73:

Verse 1: The psalmist begins his prayer of complaint with a statement of faith regarding God's character. A confession of trust is consistent in psalms that cry for help.
Verses 15-17: The psalmist vents his feelings but he avoids accusing God to others. Instead, he goes with his complaint into the presence of God
Verses 21-22: Bitterness is a barrier rather than a help.

Sources and Suggested Reading

Allender, Dan, "Feeding Your Enemy," *Discipleship Journal*, Issue 71, September/October 1992.

Allison, C. Fitzsimons, *Guilt, Anger & God*. New York: The Seabury Press, 1972.

Augsburger, David, *Caring Enough to Confront*. Ventura, Calif.: Regal Books, 1973.

_____, *Caring Enough to Forgive*. Scottsdale, Penn.: Herald Press, 1981.

_____, *Freedom of Forgiveness*. Chicago: Moody Press, 1970, 1988.

Brodin, Becky, "Helping Your Friend See God," *Discipleship Journal*, Issue 71, September/October 1992.

Fowler, Richard, "Where Is God When I Need Him," *Today's Better Life*, Premier Issue, 1991.

Harvill, Jerry, "Sticks and Stone May Break My Bones . . . ," *Discipleship Journal*, Issue 46, n.d.

Hurley, James, "Be Angry But Do Not Sin," *RTS Ministry*, Volume 10, No. 3, Fall, 1991.

Lewis, C.S., "What Are We to Make of Jesus Christ?" *God in the Dock*. Grand Rapids, Mich.: Eerdmans, 1970.

Powell, John, *Why Am I Afraid to Tell You Who I Am?* Niles, Ill.: Argus Communications, 1969.

Smedes, Lewis, "When It's Better Not to Forgive," *Marriage Partnership*, Winter, 1991.

Swindoll, Charles R., *Growing in the Seasons of Life*. Portland, Oreg.: Multnomah Press, 1983.

Wright, H. Norman, *Communication: Key to Your Marriage*. Ventura, Calif.: Regal Books, 1974.

Yancey, Philip, *Disappointment with God*. Grand Rapids, Mich.: Zondervan Publishing House, 1988.